YOUR COMPANION THROUGH CHRONIC ILLNESS

CHAPTERS BY NANCY L. LONG
DEVOTIONS BY ELIZABETH SHADBOLT

OUT OF
THE DEPTHS

Abingdon Press
Nashville

OUT OF THE DEPTHS:
YOUR COMPANION THROUGH CHRONIC ILLNESS

Copyright © 2018 by Abingdon Press

This book is printed on acid-free paper.

978-1-5018-7136-8

18 19 20 21 22 23 24 25 26 27—10 9 8 7 6 5 4 3 2 1

MANUFACTURED IN THE UNITED STATES OF AMERICA

CONTENTS

CONTENTS

INTRODUCTION

This little book is intended to be a companion through the ups and downs, twists and turns of chronic illness. It is organized into two parts. The first is educational. In it, we will consider the many ways chronic illness can affect our physical, emotional, social, and spiritual needs. It is our sincere hope that this knowledge will provide a useful framework within which to navigate your personal experience of living with chronic illness.

The second part of the book is devotional and consists of thirty daily scripture readings, devotions, and prayers. It is our sincere prayer that these readings will bring hope and comfort, provide a daily grounding faith ritual, and lend a sense of connectedness, both to God and to a community of individuals walking a similar path, as you move through the days and weeks to come. You do not have to read the first part of this book before beginning the devotions. Feel free to start them at any time.

Before we dive in, we want to let you know what you can and can't expect from this book.

This book cannot replace a medical or mental health practitioner. (Please follow the recommendations of your treatment team.)

This book cannot give you a diagnosis. (Only medical professionals give diagnoses.)

This book cannot "fix" you. (You're not broken.)

This book can empower you by educating you about living with chronic illness.

This book can provide hope when hope seems absent or distant.

This book can journey with you through the shadows and valleys, highs and lows of life with chronic illness.

If this little book has found its way into your hands, please know that we are deeply sorry. Chronic illness is, by definition, life-altering. However, even though our deepest struggles cannot be repaired, they can be redeemed; even if you cannot be healed, you can be made whole. It is our greatest hope and the crux of the Christian story that when all feels lost, God's redemptive power is already at work. Others have traveled this road before you, and one day you will become a companion who guides and blesses others as they travel through this all-too familiar valley themselves.

Grace and peace,
Nancy Long & Elizabeth Shadbolt

Chapter One
WHAT IS CHRONIC ILLNESS?

While expert definitions of "chronic illness" vary widely, chronic illness is generally understood to be a disease or condition lasting longer than three months.[1] Many chronic illnesses are life-long and incurable. Some chronic illnesses, such as diabetes and multiple sclerosis, are ongoing, and some, such as migraine headaches or recurrent hip pain, are episodic and persistent. Simply put, a chronic illness or condition is one that is not going to go away, at least not any time soon.

Chronic illness is defined in contrast to "acute" illnesses, such as the flu or a stomach virus. Acute illnesses generally have a beginning and an end and often can be treated with medicine, surgery, or other treatment protocol. For example, when you get a sinus infection, your doctor can prescribe antibiotics that kill the troublesome bacteria. Your symptoms subside, and the illness concludes. This, unfortunately, is not typically the case with chronic illnesses. As such, learning that you have (and will continue to have) a chronic illness can be a devastating experience.

Perhaps your diagnosis experience sounds like what I have heard from many of my chronically ill patients. Usually it goes something like this:

It was a beautiful, sunny day. The sky was indescribably blue and the temperature a balmy 74 degrees with a slight wind that brushed across the face. The grass was beginning to turn a luscious green. (The "before" picture is always beautiful in hindsight.)

That morning, I received a phone call from my doctor's office. They were ready to share the results of the most recent series of tests. I hurried to get the doctor's office to get the results, waiting anxiously when I arrived. The doctor stepped into the exam room and quickly got to the point. The results confirmed that I have a chronic disease. Suddenly, that seemingly perfect day turned into my worst nightmare.

I tried to regain my composure and remember the verses I learned in Vacation Bible School, but the news was so heavy I couldn't contain my emotions. What was I going to do now? Would life ever be the same? Was I going to be able to take care of myself? And what about my family? I was launched into a swirling pot of anxiety and fear and had to remind myself to breathe.

Does this sound like your experience? Or perhaps the lead up to your diagnosis was more dramatic; instead of a long series of appointments and vague test results, your condition landed you in an acute episode requiring immediate hospital care. Maybe you had been exhibiting mysterious symptoms for a long time or had been waiting to be diagnosed with the genetic condition so tragically familiar to your family.

No matter your story, you are not alone. Every day, many adults and children are diagnosed with incurable, chronic illnesses. In fact, over 40 percent (133 million) of adults in the United States are afflicted with some form of chronic disease, and this number is expected to rise dramatically in coming years. The number of individuals with multiple chronic conditions is also increasing; nearly one-third of people in the United States deal with multiple chronic issues.[2]

Chronic illness isn't unusual, but it may be new to you. It's not likely to be a welcome acquaintance. You may feel a range of emotions at your diagnosis: fear of the unknown, relief at finally having answers, concern for the people close to you, dread of prescribed treatment...there is no right or wrong way to feel about your diagnosis. Some people even find they have emotions that seem to contradict each other. That's okay, too. Take each feeling as it comes; even the more negative ones may have something to teach you. Feelings of fear, guilt, loss, anger, frustration, sadness, and grief can become toxic and lead to further health complications if not expressed in a healthy manner. Even if you are not comfortable discussing your feelings, it is vital to acknowledge those feelings. Listen to your body. It will be your constant companion throughout this journey. Even when you feel like you are fighting against it, it will be with you, through the ups and downs of this journey of life with chronic illness.

Chapter Two

MYTHS ABOUT CHRONIC ILLNESS

Because of the social stigmas that accompany chronic disease, many people shy away from discussing their concerns, fears, and anxiety about their future with anyone. The possibility of being misunderstood, having profound feelings of failure, being exposed as not having enough faith, being perceived as being punished for some unforgiven sin, feeling embarrassment, and even hopelessness are generally the reasons for not seeking help. In a society that idolizes physical health and looks down on weakness, misinformation about chronic illness abounds. Below are some common myths. Consider how you might have internalized some of these negative messages and then think about what corrective messages you might want to send yourself of those around you.

1. *Myth: Illness is a sign of God's displeasure with you.*

   In the Sermon on the Mount, Jesus explains to his listeners that the same laws of nature or society apply to everybody:

   > You have heard that it was said, "Love your neighbor and hate your enemy." But I tell you, love your enemies and pray for those who persecute you, that you may be children of your Father in heaven. He causes his sun to rise on the evil and the good and sends rain on the righteous and the unrighteous. (Matt 5:43-45)

It's the opposite of the idea that good things happen to good people and bad things happen to bad people. Chronic illness strikes both "good" people and "bad" people. There is no justice in it; it is just a fact of nature. While it can be natural and sometimes, in the short term, comforting to look for explanations and answers to "why is this happening to me" questions, the witness of scripture, in this passage and many others, is that God is not a sky-dwelling scorekeeper smiting people when their "goodness" falls below an acceptable level. Chronic illnesses affect people from all stages and walks of life.

God did not cause your illness. Rather, God is a faithful companion with you as you live into the reality of a life that will be changed (for better and for worse) by your diagnosis and condition. God is not punishing you. God grieves and celebrates and fumes along with you. God will sustain you, no matter what lies ahead.

2. *Myth: It's your own fault.*

While it's true that some chronic illnesses are brought on or exacerbated by particular actions and lifestyle choices, many are not. For example, a multiple sclerosis patient didn't bring on his or her condition by exercising too much or too little, eating the wrong foods, or so on. Some things just happen through the complex interaction of internal and external biological, genetic, physical, and environmental factors.

Behavioral choices do play a role in the development of some chronic conditions. For example, someone with a history of smoking is more likely to experience respiratory illnesses like COPD (chronic obstructive pulmonary disease). Even so, you did not make yourself sick. You did not wake up one morning and say, "I think I'll go to the store today and pick up some respiratory distress." If you smoked, your actions likely contributed to your current state of health, but you cannot draw a straight line between your choice to smoke (or engage in any other risky behavior) and the development of your illness and the resulting difficulties. It may be necessary to offer yourself forgiveness for the ways you did actively participate in less-than-ideal behaviors. We don't make our choices in a vacuum; an entire industry attempts to convince us to do, say, or use certain things. Give yourself grace.

3 *Myth: It's all in your head.*

This myth pops up most frequently in regard to conditions that cause invisible symptoms such as pain or fatigue. Because there is not definitive test or definition for conditions such as these, it can be easy for us and those around us to minimize their existence. Sometimes even clear, visible, physical symptoms are attributed to psychosomatic causes and dismissed. Doing so invalidates your lived experience and can make you question yourself: Is it all in my head? Am I overreacting? Is what I feel real? Such questioning can be crazy-making.

You are the definitive expert in your own experience. If you hurt, you hurt. If you are to-the-bone exhausted, you are exhausted, no matter what someone else might say. If you are encountering this sort of dismissal from your medical team, it may be time to shop around. If you are sending yourself these messages, go easy on yourself. Trust your mind and your body. You know you best.

4. *Myth: There's a simple solution you're missing.*

This is the myth we most wish were true. Wouldn't it be great if there were a pill or a procedure you could take or undergo that would make your condition go away and your life go back to how it was? While we should never give up hope for a cure or life-restoring treatment for our conditions, we can focus those hopes on evidence-based treatment options or tried-and-true complementary medical tactics. If the most recent fad could solve your issues easily, it wouldn't be a secret to modern medicine. Chronic diseases are almost always complex and often multi-faceted, affecting many parts or systems of the body. Many have been studied extensively (though some "orphan" conditions have been somewhat neglected in scientific interest).

Once you have developed a treatment team that you trust, let that team use its expertise. Equip and educate yourself as much as possible, but know that chances are high that the product your friend from grade school is selling isn't likely to be your miracle cure. And while prayer can be an essential practice and tool for dealing with your condition, connecting with God, and grounding yourself in the love and grace of God, prayer by itself is usually not the cure we dream about. Implicit in the emphasis that well-meaning, faithful friends and faith communities may place on the absolute power of prayer is an assumption that if only you would pray more or better, you would be relieved of your disease. In fact, your illness has nothing to do

with the quality of your character or faith practices.
(See myth #1 and Matt 22:34-40.)

5. *Myth: My life will never be the same.*

Having a chronic condition affects your life; there is
no denying it. However, it can be tempting to fall into
the trap that nothing about your life will stay the same.
When receiving an overwhelming diagnosis and dealing
with the barrage of emotions that comes with it, our
thinking can get myopic and focus only on what we
can't do or what we will lose. In fact, most people, with
proper treatment, are able to continue working, enjoy
time with family, engage in their hobbies, and so on.
As diseases progress, it is likely that you will face more
and more limitations and have to grieve many losses
along the way, but all is not lost immediately. There is
still much life to be lived . . . it just now may have to
be lived in a different way. Rather than assuming it all
must change, experiment and see which of the activities
you enjoy the most can be adapted and maintained.

6. *Myth: Nobody will want to be with me now.*

Perhaps the most vile and consistent companion to a
chronic illness diagnosis is isolation. When your life is
changing, when you become aware of more limitations,
when you require more support, and when you are
acutely aware that you don't know what the future
holds, friends and acquaintances may seem to scatter.
Living with chronic illness can be lonely. However,
those who know you, love you, and know how to show
their care may become even closer. One of the hidden
gifts of any difficult life situation is that you often
find out who your best and truest friends are. This

clarification can serve you well, particularly when you are faced with limited resources or energy.

We will discuss relationships with your loved ones more thoroughly in subsequent chapters. For now, know that you are still the same person you were before. Your diagnosis has not changed you one bit. While your ability to work, perform, or parent may be affected by your condition, you are still the same beautiful child of God that you were yesterday and will be tomorrow. This is the you that your loved ones care about; this is the you that isn't going anywhere. Even though circumstances may change, you are still beloved, loved, and wanted.

Now that we have considered what chronic illness is and is not, we turn to the question of how you will choose to live with your condition.

Chapter Three

LEARNING TO THRIVE

Living with a chronic illness has been described as one of the most difficult paths anyone can walk. Chronic disease can have a devasting impact on the emotional, physical, and spiritual aspects of your life. Just knowing the possibility that you will have to thrive with the disease or pain for the remainder of your life can be an enormous burden to carry. But it is one you can choose how to hold. Now that you have been given this devastating news, you can choose to either live with the chronic illness or look for ways to thrive while chronically ill. Living with chronic illness can be different than thriving.

In either case, your first task is facing the disclosure or revelation of the diagnosis. The news generally is unexpected and more than likely overwhelming. It is typical to have a sense of powerlessness in the beginning. As you learn to live with the realities of your current situation, you'll begin facing the prospect of a future filled with plenty of unknowns. You may be lonely and exhausted and experiencing physical and emotion pain. You may ask questions: How will my disease affect my life in years to come? How will the disease progress? Will other symptoms arise? Could my life be shortened by the illness? What effect will it have on the people I love?

It can be easy to get lost in the fear and anxiety. No wonder many people who deal with chronic illness experience depression and anxiety secondary to their primary diagnosis! Even so, many doctors overlook the emotional toll chronic illness can take on a patient and his or her family or communities. (If you are experiencing overwhelming depression or anxiety, you may be helped by the title in this series called *Out of the Depths: Your*

Companion through Depression and Anxiety. If you are feeling hopeless or like you would like to die, please contact your treatment team as soon as possible.) Managing the numerous day-to-day symptoms of chronic illness must include accepting and dealing with the flood of emotions that accompany the diagnosis, and day-to-day struggles, of chronic illness.

While feelings of depression, anxiety, fear, sadness, anger, or hopelessness may seem overwhelming and exhausting, a passive approach to your illness may not be what serves you best. Learning to thrive with a chronic illness requires intentional effort and necessitates reliance on resources you may not have realized you had at your disposal. Whether you are going to live with your diagnosis or thrive in the midst of it is, in large part, up to you. While there is much about your disease you cannot control, you can control your attitude and approach to it.

As noted in the introduction to this book, you are not broken. Your body has limitations. Your mind may not function as well, quickly, or sharply as it once did. There may be things you flat out cannot do, even activities of daily living. Even so, you are a full and complete being, a beloved child of God. As Paul encourages his young friend Timothy, "Don't let anyone look down on you because you are young [or old or sick or ill or have arthritis or diabetes or are in pain or, or, or...]. Instead, set an example for the believers through your speech, behavior, love, [and] faith" (1 Tim 4:12). Even with your limitations, God is not done with you yet. Give yourself grace, but don't sell yourself short.

You are still you. You are of value to society. You are someone who can contribute, despite whatever limitations you may possess. All of us humans have limitations. Yours may be more obvious than others, but none of us is all-powerful. You deserve to be seen as a full and complete person by others and by yourself. Remind yourself when you feel less than, that you are quite capable of many things.

One myth we didn't consider in the previous chapter I hear patients telling themselves is, "I'm not able." Certainly, your capabilities may have changed, but there is still much you can do. Think about what gifts and abilities you now possess. There may be ways to act, serve, and help that are new to you in the context of your illness. Are you more compassionate? More empathetic? Have more time to listen or write cards? Are you more aware of others' needs? Have you found a way to transform your pain through creativity that enriches the world?

Chapter Four

LIVING YOUR BEST LIFE

Our society can make it easy to believe that someone who is different than we are has different basic human needs. Whether a person is chronically ill or has a broken leg or is going through a divorce, he or she never loses his or her social needs (for connection: love, belonging, partnership, communication), emotional needs (for peace: inner peace, hope, balance, forgiveness), existential needs (for meaning and purpose: meaning in life, self-actualization, role function) and spiritual needs (for transcendence: relationship with God or the sacred, prayer, spiritual practices, an understanding of the context of suffering). While your physical needs may be drastically altered because of chronic illness, the bulk of the rest of your needs remain intact in a way similar to those before your diagnosis. Because of your newfound limitations, you may not be able to meet your needs through the same methods you employed in the past. For example, regularly attending a worship service can fulfill social, emotional, existential, and spiritual needs…but your physical limitations prohibit regular attendance. You will need to work with your treatment team to develop ways to address these unmet needs within the framework of your new reality. Perhaps a pastor or regular visitor who can study the Bible and pray with you might help meet your needs. Maybe you are able to stream the worship service online, which could meet some (though not all) of your needs. When life brings limitations or a change in circumstances, we must be creative in finding ways to live our best lives in spite of (and perhaps through!) the changes. Below are some ways that my patients have refocused and reshaped their lives as they adjust to having a chronic illness. As with any suggestions, take what works for you and leave the rest.

STAY CONNECTED

Beyond the physical issues, perhaps the most difficult and pervasive challenge chronic illness presents is the risk of isolation. Circumstances around our illness can cut us off from communities of which we were regularly a part. If you can't participate in former hobbies, aren't as mobile as you used to be, or are frequently battling physical symptoms, social activities outside of your home are more complicated. Perhaps your illness has caused you to stop working. Depending on the nature of your work environment, the loss of your work community may trigger significant grief. These feelings are normal, natural, and worth feeling. Likewise, you may feel grief when friends and acquaintances share what they've been doing because it can emphasize the loss of control that you have suffered. Still, as you are ready, hearing about others' adventures will allow you to feel connected to the world.

While circumstances can isolate us from people, our own choices can, too. In high-stress or transitional times, withdrawing and keeping to yourself or your very closest circles can be tempting. It takes effort to explain your situation over and over again, to manage other people's anxieties around it, and to chronicle each step of your journey to catch people up. With limited energy and resources, of course you'd want to spend most of your time with those closest to you who already know the answers to all the questions, or maybe you feel like it's easiest just to be alone and deal with your emotions and symptoms on your own, or worse yet, to choose not to deal with your emotions. However, in the long run, this sort of approach will not sure you well. You certainly get to choose who you share your time and story with, but challenge yourself to keep connecting beyond the folks you see every day. Choose wisely, but try to keep your support system broad so that when one part of your network is unavailable, you will have others to draw from. Besides, as we noted above, your needs haven't changed. You still need friends, and your friends still love and need you in their lives, too. Try not to feed your sense of isolation by withdrawing.

While your chronic illness may pose challenges to maintaining your relationships, it might open doors to new connections. Depending on the nature of your illness, you may be meeting many new people upon your diagnosis. Even though doctors, nurses, and therapists are not the same as close friends you can call at any hour, they can provide a wealth of support and compassion. Some deep friendships have been forged with other patients in waiting rooms. Check with your hospital or treatment center about ongoing support groups. In-person friendships and relationships will always be important, though many chronic illness patients have found great support in online communities. Even folks who live far away but have similar struggles can become close friends. (Of course, use common sense when engaging in online communities and don't share sensitive personal information.)

We all need the love and attention of other people. Chronic illness, by its nature, is incredibly isolating. Don't go it alone.

LISTEN TO YOUR BODY

As we noted in chapter 1, your body will be your one constant companion through your journey of chronic illness. When your body isn't performing how you would like it to or various portions of it are in constant pain, it's easy to see it as your enemy. Your body refuses to cooperate and is the source of your limitations. Each day may feel like another battle: you versus your body.

However, our bodies and spirits are not so easily separated. We are embodied people; that is, our bodies are essential to who we are, rather than simply being a vessel for our souls. A wearied and broken body can easily yield a weary and broken soul...but it doesn't have to be that way. Can you imagine that your body might be a being to befriend rather than an obstacle to overcome? How might you work together with your body to improve your life with your illness? How can you learn to accept your body with all its flaws and foibles?

Likely each time you visit a care provider you will be asked about your pain level and any changes in symptoms. Such symptoms can be a nuisance and downright painful and tiresome, but our symptoms can also be clues teaching us about our disease process. Take a careful inventory of your symptoms and physical sensations. Do you see patterns? Have some subsided while others increased? Sharing such information with your doctor can help chart the course of your treatment, but it can also help you stay in touch with your body.

Our bodies have much to tell us, physically and emotionally. Without realizing it, we carry many emotions in our bodies themselves. Have you ever sensed butterflies in your stomach when you were nervous? Or felt like a weight is pushing down on your chest when you've been anxious or afraid? Maybe you feel a warmth in your chest when you hug someone close to you.

So much of the treatment of chronic illness is focused on the physical symptoms that emotional signals can get lost. Doing a meditative body scan is one way to reconnect your body and spirit. Meditation instructor Elaine Smookler writes,

Regularly practicing the body scan can help you:

Enhance your ability to bring your full attention to real-time experiences happening in the present moment—helpful when emotions or thoughts feel wild.

Train to explore and be with pleasant *and* unpleasant sensations, learning to notice what happens when we simply hang in there and feel what's going on in "body-land" without trying to fix or change anything.[1]

To do a basic body scan meditation, find a position that is most comfortable and balanced for you (sitting, lying, or even standing). Close your eyes if you are comfortable doing so or fix your gaze in the middle distance without distractions. Breathing deeply and slowly, start at the top of your head and note any sensations you feel, whether they be pain, buzzing, throbbing, warming, swirling, shaking, and so on. There's no need to analyze or judge the sensation; simply make a note of it. Try to keep your attention on your body. If your mind drifts, gently bring your attention back to your breath and your body. Continue to scan for sensations, slowly, all the way through your body and to your toes. When you are finished, take a few more slow, deep breaths; open your eyes; and bring your attention back to the room around you. As you practice this gentle meditation more and more, you may notice patterns. Does your body seem to hold a certain sensation or emotion in a particular part? How might this be related to your illness? Let your body be your guide, not your adversary.

KEEP LAUGHING

You've heard the cliché that laughter is the best medicine. Proverbs gives us similar advice in 17:22: "A joyful heart help healing, but a broken spirit dries up the bones." We have talked extensively about the significant grief process that accompanies a chronic illness diagnosis. Sometimes, though, you've just got to laugh.

In coming to terms with a chronic illness diagnosis, acceptance is the first step. Accepting one's current circumstances can feel impossible at first. You are justified in feeling angry, hurt, and unfairly treated by God and life. Keeping your sense of humor can help you move toward acceptance. Your illness and circumstances are not a joke, but life has a lot to laugh about in spite of your diagnosis. When the pressure from fear, anxiety, anger, and frustration has built up, one healthy release is through laughter. A sense of relief comes in the form of a merry heart. This doesn't mean anyone has the right to disrespect you or minimize your difficult experience. Instead, humor can be a way of removing yourself from the center of your illness and seeing that the world is more than your diagnosis. Laughter can bring perspective.

Put yourself in the company of people who are funny and have a positive attitude about their circumstances. Watch more comedy and less news. Remember funny stories passed down through your family, read blogs and listen to podcasts with a lighthearted tone, gently poke fun at yourself as appropriate. Even when if it seems impossible to do, or unlikely to help, laughter really does do a body good.

HELP OTHERS HELP YOU: ADVOCATE FOR YOURSELF MEDICALLY

You will encounter numerous and varied experts tending to every facet of your chronic condition. They will have many degrees and extensive experience. They will be full of knowledge, facts, and hopefully, compassion. But they will not live in your body. They will not inhabit your mind. They will not study your every moment of every day the way that you will live with yourself. You are the expert on you and your experience and you should be a valuable part of the treatment team. Inform yourself about your illness by researching reputable sites and reading material from your doctor's office. Track your symptoms so you can communicate your experience to your doctor. Take a friend or family member with you to appointments so that he or she can hear what the doctor says and ensure you are communicating everything you want to say to the doctor. Encourage your doctors to talk directly with each other when collaborating in your care. Finally, if you aren't feeling listened to by your treatment team, don't be afraid to seek out care elsewhere. You deserve to be heard.

HELP OTHERS HELP YOU:
TELL YOUR STORY (IF YOU WANT)

If you live or worship in a tight-knit community, you know that information—and misinformation—can spread rapidly. And since you are likely highly involved in the medical system these days, you know that HIPPA (the Health Insurance Portability and Accountability Act of 1996) protects private health information from being shared with people outside your treatment team without your consent. Given that many of us participate in at least one form of social media, you know that sharing information about yourself is easier than ever. Taken together, this means that if you have a story to tell, you can tell it without much logistical trouble. Still, the diagnosis and journey of life with chronic illness remains *your* story to tell—if and when and how you want to.

We all have varying levels of comfort with sharing personal information, and that's perfectly appropriate. What's important is knowing what *you* want to share about yourself, which may change over time. Having an "elevator speech" of one to two minutes about your condition and how it affects your life may be helpful and can fend off overly probing questions. On the other hand, some people find sharing their story, ups and downs, and feelings on a personal blog beneficial. Most people share different amounts and levels of information and emotions appropriate to the depth of the relationship. The one constant is that you are the one who can accurately describe your experience. Still, if you are not a particularly expressive person or when you don't necessarily understand what is going on in your body, sharing others' descriptions of your illness and life with it may be the method of educating the people around you. Many common chronic conditions have research and fundraising organizations with highly developed websites, including disease descriptions and personal testimonies of living with the disease.

Your story is your story. Nobody can tell it like you. You decide when, if, and how you want to tell it. At the same time, not sharing your story can limit the extent to which others can be a part of it.

HELP OTHERS HELP YOU: STATE YOUR NEEDS

Generally, people really do want to help. You may encounter somewhat misguided attempts at assistance such as people making assumptions about what you are and aren't capable of doing on your own. Such attempts to help may feel uncomfortable or patronizing. Try to sense the positive intent behind the helper's actions and steer them in a more helpful direction. Everyone's circumstances are unique. You know best what would help you. Maybe it's helping with light cleaning around the house, transportation to and from appointments, regular greeting cards in the mail, or a night out with friends. When a friend asks how they can help, don't be shy; be honest about how he or she can assist you in the most effective way, physically and emotionally. Different relationships will call for different needs to be addressed, but making a list of possible ways for people to step in can help you learn to accept and guide your loved ones' care and compassion.

LEAN ON YOUR SPIRITUAL RESOURCES

Your journey with chronic illness will no doubt challenge and frustrate you at times. In these times of difficulty, you will need to draw on the rich spiritual resources within and around you to get through. If you are a part of a faith community, even if you have not been active, avail yourself of their support and resources. Reach out to the pastor(s). It's easy to assume that she or he knows what is going on but unless someone tells the pastor, there's no way for her or him to find out! Perhaps your church or faith community has a Stephen Minister program or a special visitation pastor. Many communities host support groups of various kinds, and some churches may be able to help with material or financial needs. Trust the community to care for you, but let them know you need it.

Engage in spiritual practices that give you life. Participate in worship as you are able, whether it's by physically attending, watching online or on TV, or listening to CDs or podcasts of recent services and sermons. Journaling can be a helpful way to check in with yourself spiritually; it can also open you up to God's care and voice. Reading or meditating on scripture can be meaningful. The book of Psalms is a particularly rich part of the Bible to dive into. In it, the Hebrew people express the full range of human emotions and offer it to God in the context of praise. The modern-day psalms of music and poetry have gotten many people through dark times. Consider making use of a daily devotional as a part of your routine.

While your body's limitations may prevent you from participating in your faith community and many spiritual activities, you always have the ability to pray. Even when we can't find the words, Romans tells us, "the Spirit comes to help our weakness. We don't know what we should pray, but the Spirit himself pleads our case with unexpressed groans" (8:26). Pray for understanding and peace to handle what life has dealt you. Pray not just for healing but for strength to endure. Hold the members of your treatment team in God's light... heaven knows you want them to have as much wisdom as possible!

Most of all, remember that God is with you and will never leave or forget you. Life in a human body can be hard, more so when that body's functioning is somehow impaired. But God remains within and with you. As Ann Voskamp writes, "The Jesus I know never preached some health-prosperity Gospel, some pseudo-good news that if you just pray well, sing well, worship well, live well and deposit all that into some Divine ATM—you get to take home a mind and body that are well. That's not how the complex beauty of life unfolds."[2] No, the "complex beauty of life" unfolds one day, one struggle, one appointment, one diagnosis, one pill, and one chuckle at a time. And through each one, the God who created the vast universe one infinitesimal particle at a time will remain by your side.

Devotions for Living
with Chronic Illness

GEARING UP

Pick up the full armor of God. . . . Stand with the belt of truth around your waist, justice as your breastplate, and put shoes on your feet. . . . Take the helmet of salvation and the sword of the Spirit, which is God's word.
—*Ephesians 6:14-17*

In his letter to the new Christians in Ephesus, Paul uses battle imagery, specifically about the battle between good and evil. As you begin your journey with a chronic illness, you may also feel that you are preparing for battle and in many ways, you are. Over the coming days and months, you will need to advocate for yourself, navigate many choices and options, and create healthy boundaries that allow you space to rest and heal. Think about the "full armor of God" that Paul describes—some items are for protection like a breastplate and shoes. The shield is for defense and the sword of the Spirit is what we have for attack.

But this isn't a sword forged from steel. This sword is the word of God. Throughout our time together, we will delve into God's word, unwrap the promises God has made, seek out comfort from the scripture, and create new habits of prayer. As we gear up, what parts of this armor are you already wearing? What do you need to fortify for the days ahead? Which of these have been difficult for you in the past? Together, we'll start this journey and find ways to feed our souls and sustain us for whatever may come.

Imagine yourself wearing the armor of God. Perhaps your shoes are bunny slippers instead of boots. Maybe your sword looks more like an IV pole. Where or what would truth, justice, faith, salvation, and the Spirit be? Tuck this image away to pull out on difficult days.

WHEN LIFE ISN'T GOING AS PLANNED

I know the plans I have in mind for you, declares the LORD; they are plans for peace, not disaster, to give you a future filled with hope.
—Jeremiah 29:11

There are a million clichés about life being a journey. Few of them seem helpful when you are diagnosed with a serious illness. "Life is a journey, not a destination" seems saccharine at best when you are re-thinking what your future will look like and wondering how you will get through the present. "Escape the ordinary" is just a punch to the gut when all you long for is what was once "ordinary." When our abilities to fulfill our dreams and goals for the future are put into question, our hearts and minds can become black holes of worry. The danger of falling into a spiral of fear becomes all too real.

This verse from Jeremiah reminds us that God is the creator of life and that we are part of the plans God has made for the world. These words were written to the Jews while they were exiled in Babylon. God encouraged them to go about their lives, to do what's necessary and continue to pray. God promised to bring them out of captivity and return them to the promised land. Our health statuses may be out of our control, but God is not veering from plans for our future. Just as God stayed true to the promise made to the exiled Israelites, so will God stay true to us. Jeremiah reminds us that in times of uncertainty and doubt, we can lean into the promise that God is in control.

Allow your mind to rest. See what words of hope and comfort come to mind. As you breath in, speak one of those words. As you breath out, speak another. Allow your words of hope and comfort to sink into your soul.

MIXED FEELINGS

Come near to God, and he will come near to you.

—James 4:8

Being diagnosed with a chronic illness brings a huge and over-whelming bag of feelings, often mixed. Many people have been suffering for months, years, even decades before a diagnosis can be made or a treatment plan can begin. We've gone through doctor's appointments, tests, all kinds of blood work, and the interminable waiting that goes along with all of that. The phrase "stumbling through the darkness" describes this journey well. But, as frightening as a diagnosis can be, it can also bring welcomed relief: there is a name; there is research; there are treatments. And, with those answers will come more waiting...cue the emotional roller-coaster.

While we journey through these feelings, we remember that God brings us words of hope and comfort. What were the words that came to mind in yesterday's reading? Can those divinely inspired words offer you peace and security as you ride this roller coaster? God seeks to be with us both in joy and in trial. It's up to us to find ways to let God in. Make space to feel all that you are feeling, and ask for God's presence and direction as you move forward. Know that the stars were set for you by God's loving hand; they shine in your darkness.

Lord, I need your abiding presence to calm and comfort me today.
My emotions catch me off-guard, and I don't always know how to
process them. Be with me, Lord, as I question and doubt. Be with
me as I give thanks. Guide me in this darkness, for I know that
your hand is sure. Amen.

A PILGRIMAGE SONG

*The LORD will protect you on your journeys—whether going or coming—
from now until forever from now.*

—Psalm 121:7-8

I love the Psalms. They were written centuries ago by people known and unknown in places and situations that we can only imagine, and yet the Psalms speak to us through the ages. They express our joy and thankfulness, they speak of our trials and despair, they help us wait on the Lord. Psalm 121 is often considered a "pilgrimage" song, as its language evokes the exodus journey. Several times throughout the passage, we are reminded that God will "keep" and "guard" us, not just now but "forever from now."

My youngest son contracted walking pneumonia a few days before the first day of kindergarten. He'd never been so sick before, and he was devastated to miss such an important day. For several nights, he slept in my bed and had feverish dreams, every so often flopping out his left had to take hold of me or my pajamas. Once he had hold, his face would calm, his breathing would slow, and he would sleep deeply. As much as I hated that he was suffering, it gave me joy to be his comfort and protection. I imagine that our creator feels that way about us. When God sees us flailing for help, God's desire is for us to find a hold and accept the comfort.

Imagine the voice of God comforting you right now. What words of hope do you need to hear? What words of protection would give you rest? Breathe these words in as you cultivate this loving inner voice.

WHAT'S THE WEATHER LIKE?

*Certainly the faithful love of the LORD hasn't ended; certainly God's
compassion isn't through! They are renewed every morning.*
— Lamentations 3:22-23

You may have grown up in a household that eschewed dinner time talk about religion or politics, which could leave weather as the only safe subject. My grandparents talked about and worried about the weather incessantly, likely due to their days working the family farm in Iowa. At my kitchen table, our family discusses many things—and doesn't shy away from religion and politics—but it has always been hard to get my boys to talk about their feelings. So instead, I ask about the weather, outside and in.

Sometimes the outside weather is cloudy and grey, leading to our "inside weather" also being heavy and morose. Sometimes we have a light mood that matches a bright, spring day. Other times, our internal weather may contrast severely, causing us to pull the curtains tight and climb into bed. Those are difficult days. Those are days that I experience "FOMO"—the Fear Of Missing Out. When I know that people are out enjoying a lovely day, doing the things I love to do but am unable to, it's hard to remember that a new day will come. These words from Lamentations remind us that we can rest well knowing that God's mercies are renewed each morning.

*Lord, hold me as I take time to rest. Bless my friends and family
as they go and do even though I may not be able to join them. My
heart is glad at the memories of past times together, and I know
that, thanks to your grace, there will be new memories to feast on
later. Amen.*

ADJUSTING TO THE WIND

[Jesus] got up and gave orders to the wind and the violent waves.
The storm died down and it was calm.

—*Luke 8:24*

When my husband and I were first married, my brother-in-law sold us his sailboat for a dollar. It was a deal we couldn't resist, and we spent many summer afternoons enjoying our investment on the lake. I didn't have much experience with sailing, but my husband had learned as a camp counselor. It was fascinating to watch him adjust the sails of our tiny boat to catch the wind that was blowing all around us. I could feel it stinging my skin, but didn't know how to capture it to propel us smoothly across the water. The same can be true when you are navigating your new life with chronic illness. So much information, so many opinions, so many decisions swirl around us. In the confusion it can be difficult to ascertain just how to go in the right direction. As the saying goes, "We cannot direct the wind, but we can adjust the sails."

In Luke 8, Jesus and his disciples are in a boat on the sea of Galilee when a storm suddenly rises. As the waves crash against the boat and the winds howl, the disciples panic. After Jesus gets up from his nap and calms the storm, "he said to his disciples, 'Where is your faith?' Filled with awe and wonder, they said to each other, 'Who is this? He commands even the winds and the water, and they obey him!'" (Luke 8:25). Jesus can calm the most terrifying wind, but we must remain faithful. And how do we remain faithful? Writer Rachel Held Evans puts it well: "Faith is about following the quiet voice of God without having everything figured out ahead of time."[1]

Jesus, we ask for you daily to calm the storms around us, to help us catch the wind that will send us in the right direction. Strengthen our faith so, trusting in your plan, we can hear your quiet voice. Amen.

CHOICES

Even when I walk through the darkest valley...you are with me.
—*Psalm 23:4*

Part of what makes the journey through chronic illness so difficult is the lack of choice. We don't get to choose a diagnosis or a set of symptoms. We don't get to choose how those things will impact our lives or our relationships. Feeling the loss of agency and independence is another part of the grief we must process. These feelings are real and need to be acknowledged!

So what choices are left when your health puts you at your lowest? Michael J. Fox affirms that while we can't choose whether we have a chronic illness, "surrounding that non-choice is a million other choices that [we] can make."[2] Such choices include choosing to feel your feelings rather than push them aside, and choosing to allow even the scary thoughts to be addressed. Rumi, the ancient Sufi mystic, wrote in his opening lines to "The Guest House" that "this being human is a guest house." He goes on to invite the reader to treat these newly arriving feelings like honored guests. "Welcome and entertain them all!" whether they be good, bad, happy or sad. Rumi reminds us that these "visitors" are sent from God, from the great beyond. Our emotions are just one way that we connect with the great enormity of God.

When we welcome and honor all of our feelings, we are freed to make choices, big and small. Today, the choice may be which physician to visit or which protocol to follow. Tomorrow the choice may be which pajamas to wear and which tea to drink. By honoring all of our emotions on this journey, we free our hearts and minds to follow God's intention for our lives.

Take a moment to acknowledge a feeling you are having—perhaps one that is gnawing away with neglect or shame. Honor and embrace it. Pray love and compassion over it. Each feeling is part of what makes you whole and has something to teach you.

NATURE HEALS

Consider the ravens: they neither plant nor harvest, they have no silo or barn, yet God feeds them. You are worth so much more than birds!
—Luke 12:24

Near our home is a wonderful city park: hidden in between some lovely hills is a small pond teeming with wildlife, hiking paths, a paved walking trail, and wildflowers galore. We've been to this park in every season of the year and in many seasons of our life, hiking together, pushing babies, running after kids, strolling with our parents. One of the blessings that this park has given us in its diversity is the variety of ways to approach it. When I am feeling great, I can scale the surrounding hills and walk for miles around the water. When I am not well, I can take the paved path while my kids run and play. And there have been times when a friend has helped me to a bench, so I can enjoy the view from there alone.

The wonders of nature are truly a gift from God in their beauty and complexity. As Alice Walker wrote in *The Color Purple*, "People think pleasing God is all God cares about. But any fool living in the world can see it always trying to please us back."[3] I've always found it very healing to connect with this gift in whatever way I can, even if it's just through a window. In Luke 12, we're reminded that God has created the beauty around us even though it lasts for only a brief time. How much more must God care for us! Take a moment today to admire God's creation, to remember your connection to the earth, and to give thanks.

Lord, it's easy to take your creation for granted but when we stop to appreciate the beauty that surrounds us, we are humbled by your love. Thank you, loving God, for nourishing us through nature and for caring for us. Allow my time in your splendor to restore my soul. Amen.

JOY

Weeping may stay all night, but by morning, joy!
—*Psalm 30:5b*

When was the last time you felt pure joy? Take a moment to reflect. Nothing? Then think about the last time you experienced someone else experiencing joy. Perhaps it was a toddler burying her head in the fur of a sweet dog. Perhaps it was the first glimpse of a report card or the surprise of a rainbow. Mary Oliver instructs us in her prose poem, "Don't Hesitate," that life's surprising joys may be "its way of fighting back.... joy is not meant to be a crumb."[4] We are not meant to sweep up the crumbs of others' joy to piece together a faded remnant of the whole. Joy is ours to be had, too.

In the Bible we read stories of people worshipping God with expansive joy, a reflection of their thanks and praise. So, too, can our joy be an act of worship. Our ability to connect with joy even in difficult times is indeed an act of "fighting back." So, too, is it an act of claiming the greatness of our faith in a God who is with us even when joy feels like a crumb.

At the end of a long semester, one of our college interns came into the office and shouted, "I saw three dogs today!" In the midst of her exams and papers, the difficult field work she was doing with those experiencing homelessness, and struggles in her personal life, she saw three dogs—and it made her day. May we all be open to the joys, big and small, placed on our paths.

<hr>

Contemplate things that brought you joy in the past and compare those to things that bring you joy now. You may feel grief as you think about how things may have changed, but take time to breathe deeply, to appreciate those memories, and to think about the many joys that God has prepared for your future.

<hr>

ANGER

PUBLIC BREATHING
VERSUS PRIVATE BREATHING

Get away from me, all you evildoers, because the LORD has heard me crying! The LORD has listened to my request. The LORD accepts my prayer.
—*Psalm 6:8-9*

Grieving is a process, and just like denial, bargaining, depression, and acceptance, anger is a necessary stop on the journey. We tend to be uncomfortable with anger. It can be frightening, and it can make people uneasy. It can cause those around us to look for ways to appease and soothe, to try to quiet and cover our anger. We can feel that our anger in an inconvenience and burden, but feeling anger, instead of denying or avoiding it, moves us toward health.

In feeling our anger, we let it out, let it dissipate, and let it uncover other feelings that are even deeper in our souls. Anger is sometimes considered a "secondary emotion," meaning that there is always another emotion underneath it, often fear or hurt. Be curious about your anger. What is it trying to hide or tell you?

The God who created the heavens and the earth is strong enough to withstand our anger and help us uncover our deeper feelings. During the first few months of my diagnosis, I spent my daily commute in tears of anger. As my car merged and flowed through traffic, I felt like I could actually let my anger flow without upsetting my loved ones. Once I began taking that anger to God, I finally felt moments of relief as the anger dissipated. Sharing the emotions underlying my anger with God was much more constructive than driving and crying.

In your quiet space, re-read the scripture for today. In the heart of the Bible, the psalmist expresses fear, outrage, and anger but still knows that the Lord there. Consider ways to remember this next time anger overwhelms you.

PUBLIC BREATHING
VERSUS PRIVATE BREATHING

So how can I, my lord's servant, speak with you, my lord? Even now there's no strength in me, and I can barely breathe.

—Daniel 10:17

A natural musician, our younger son sings in a local children's choir. Knowing nothing about singing, I've learned so much from his dedicated conductors, such as the nuances of breathing musically. Sometimes when a choir sings, they all take a breath together. It may aid in the interpretation of the piece or be musically appropriate. This is a "public breath." Other times, the music needs to be sustained, so individual singers stagger their breathing in such a way that the audience doesn't perceive it. These are "private breaths." Throughout private breathing, as you take a moment to take in air, those around you continue singing.

Throughout my journey with chronic illness, I've learned the importance of utilizing private and public breaths. There are times that I can breathe publicly, asking for help, letting my needs be known, allowing myself to be vulnerable to others. But there are other times that I need to breath privately, shielding myself from whatever scorn or judgment I'm perceiving. When I need to take a private breath, my community continues its life and allows me the time I need. God continues to hold me; the Spirit remains in my company.

※※※※※※※※※※※※※※※※※※※※※※※※※

Holy Lord, you breathed into us the breath of life and continue to sustain us by your grace. Be with me as I breathe, whether it be desperate gulps of air or sighs of relief. Remind me of your presence through this most basic physical act. Amen.

※※※※※※※※※※※※※※※※※※※※※※※※※

SURRENDERING

A branch can't produce fruit by itself, but must remain in the vine.
Likewise, you can't produce fruit unless you remain in me. I am the vine;
you are the branches.

—*John 15:4-5*

The song "Never Surrender" was an anthem of my early years. I internalized the lyrics: "No one can take away your right to fight and never surrender." To surrender was to give up. It's a great song, full of early eighties synthesizer sounds and electric guitar, heartfelt singing, and a languid and intense energy. Listen to a song like this and you're ready to conquer the world and never give up! Never surrender!

When I started fighting an illness I realized how deeply these lyrics and messages like it had affected me—and how prevalent they are in our society. To surrender is to fail, yet the Bible urges us to surrender ourselves to God. We are reminded time and again that it's only through yielding to our loving God that we are truly free. As Jesus says, through surrendering our sense of control and our sense of aloneness, we can be part of the branch that produces fruit! As we journey through times of uncertainty and pain, society tells us to "keep on keeping on" but God tells us to let go. This requires an extraordinary amount of trust and takes time. It requires waiting and having confidence in God's presence and power. We live into our truest identity as a child of the living God, the one who has surrendered and keeps surrendering, by leaning into the hands that hold us eternally.

During your time of prayer, use the practice of "breath prayer" to
remind yourself to keep surrendering. As you breathe in, say "keep"
and as you breathe out, say "surrender." Allow this practice to
remind your heart that surrender to God is constant.

FRIENDS FOREVER

Continue encouraging each other and building each other up,
just like you are doing already.
—*1 Thessalonians 5:11*

Sherri was introduced to me by a mutual friend who knew we shared the same diagnosis. Our first lunch date started out a little awkwardly, but I quickly realized how much we had in common. It was reassuring to meet someone who could relate to the big and little difficulties I was encountering. Better yet, she met those things with courage and humor. I'm so glad that I went out of my comfort zone to meet a stranger and share myself with her. She continues to be an encourager and confidant. My life has been blessed abundantly through her friendship.

I truly believe God puts the people we need in our path. Think back to the people who shaped and guided you. How did you meet them? What difference did they make in your life? Now that you are dealing with a chronic illness, new or renewed connections might be helpful. We all need people we can turn to outside of our immediate family and with whom to share joy and pain. Ask your doctor's office for information on support groups in your community. Don't be afraid to look online, as well. Online friends can be part of God's plan for connection and wholeness! You are gaining valuable knowledge and experience that will allow you to lighten another person's burden down the road. We can, as John Lennon wrote, "get by with a little help from [our] friends."[5]

Take time to think about the people who you are offering support and thank God for their friendship. Where do you need more support? Ask God for guidance as you seek out those people or communities.

FRUSTRATION

In the same way, the Spirit comes to help our weakness. We know that God works all things together for good for the ones who love God, for those who are called according to his purpose.

—*Romans 8:26-28*

It was a beautiful summer day outside, but I was inside with the blinds shut, on the phone with my doctor's office. We'd just changed health insurance plans, and I was experiencing an exacerbation of my illness, one that left me barely able to function. After making an appointment for the next day, my phone rang. My appointment was cancelled. My doctor no longer took my insurance. Talk about frustration! It feels like the most frustrating things routinely happen when I feel least able to deal with them—physically, mentally, and emotionally. I'm not always able to take a step back, to inhale and exhale fully, consider my options, to reach out for help.

When Paul wrote to the Romans, he was sending letters of encouragement and strength to new Christians who were living under persecution. Paul reminds the Roman Christians that not all things in life are good for us, but even through them, God's purpose triumphs. As I look back on the frustrating day of my cancelled appointment, I can see the wheels of God's plan turning for me. I found a new doctor who really listened to me and was interested in new approaches to my care. Due to that frustrating day, I was able to chart a new course.

Take a few deep and cleansing breaths and rest in God's love for you. Think about the things that you are navigating well. Think about the challenges you have overcome thus far. Be thankful.

CENTERING YOURSELF

If anything is excellent and if anything is admirable, focus your thoughts on these things: all that is true, all that is holy, all that is just, all that is pure, all that is lovely, and all that is worthy of praise.... The God of peace will be with you.

—*Philippians 4:8-9*

f you've ever participated in a yoga class or meditation, you are familiar with the idea of "centering" oneself. To be centered is to have a calm alertness. Your mind and emotions are still, your breathing is controlled, and you are able to take note of what is going on around and inside you. This sense of centeredness can be essential to understanding or making changes necessary to live your best life. Henri Nouwen writes, "You don't think your way into a new kind of living. You live your way into a new kind of thinking."[6]

As we begin the journey with chronic illness, we expect our thoughts and emotions will often be overwhelming. Health concerns and the feelings of helplessness and grief that come with them can make it difficult to make decisions or even think through your next steps. But even in stress and illness, God's world still holds beauty and joy and "all that is worthy of praise." By cultivating practices that bring centeredness, we can better feel the presence of the God of peace on this journey with us, and in centering ourselves in the Lord, we can be reminded of the gifts we have been given that will aid us in the days ahead.

◇◇◇

Begin taking moments during the day to offer a centered time to God. It may take practice to achieve! Be patient with yourself and your busy mind.

◇◇◇

THE NEED FOR INDEPENDENCE

When pride comes, so does shame, but wisdom brings humility.
—*Proverbs 11:2*

One of the more difficult aspects of dealing with a chronic illness is the loss of independence. Having to depend on others is threatening to our sense of self. I have always been fiercely independent, and my family loves recalling some of the very first words I spoke: "Stop, Mom! I want to do it myself!" No one can remember just what it was that I wanted to do for myself, but it would be safe to guess anything and everything. Losing some independence due to my illness has been inconvenient and humbling, to say the least. At first, I found ways to do without rather than ask for help, unwilling to take a peek behind the curtain to see what was behind my urgent need for autonomy.

Our need for independence can blind us to real limitations we may be experiencing. Our desire for autonomy can lead to pride rather than freedom. Adapting to new situations shows resilience and allows us the pride of being able to do for ourselves. But doing for ourselves in order to keep our pride intact divests us from relationships with others and with God. Taking a step back to reevaluate our abilities and needs is the only way to be sure that we are putting ourselves, rather than our pride, first.

Consider this quotation from C. S. Lewis: "Pride is spiritual cancer: it eats up the very possibility of love, or contentment, or even common sense."[7] How is your pride affecting you?

SLEEPLESS NIGHTS

The LORD will fight for you. You just keep still.

—Exodus 14:14

I've never had a hard time falling asleep. My husband will tell you that all it takes is to put a movie on! It's the staying asleep that I struggle with. Once I am awake during the night, it's easy to let my mind be taken over by worries and what-ifs. During those wide-awake nights, I run like wild down the worst-case-scenario rabbit trail, imagining all of the most terrible things that might occur in the coming days. By the morning, life as we know it has ceased to exist in my imagination, and I am astounded when the sun manages to rise yet again.

In the book of Exodus, Moses is leading his people out of Egypt, but they can still see Pharaoh's troops on their heels. The Israelites are afraid that they are going to their death and their faith falters, but Moses reassures them, "The Lord will fight for you. You just keep still." Just keep still. Like a person lying awake in bed in the middle of the night. Know that the Lord will fight for you. Allow that knowledge to be the thread that links you to hope. Let this reassurance keep you through the night until the winds of worry die down.

Take a moment to commit this verse to your memory and your heart: "The Lord will fight for you. You just keep still." Create a prayer around to use when worry overtakes you. Wrap a calmness around the verse to tether yourself to hope even in the darkest times.

YOU JUST KNOW IT

Pray like this:
Our Father who is in heaven, uphold the holiness of your name.
Bring in your kingdom
so that your will is done on earth as it's done in heaven.
Give us the bread we need for today.
Forgive us for the ways we have wronged you,
just as we also forgive those who have wronged us.
And don't lead us into temptation, but rescue us from the evil one.
—Matthew 6:9-13

I taught an elementary Sunday school class that included several kids from refugee families who were just learning English. We spent many weeks learning the Lord's Prayer and worked to commit it to memory. Many months later, long after we had moved on to other lessons, one little boy was talking about feeling bullied at school. When he was upset, he told us, he liked to say the Lord's Prayer. The best part, he said, was that you didn't even have to think about it. You just know it!

There are only a few dozen words in this powerful prayer given to us by Jesus. It considers the past, present, and future, and in beautiful verse summarizes the tenets of our faith. In the preceding verses, Jesus warns against "showy" religion and prayer. He chastises people who use too many words when they pray. "Don't be like them, because your Father knows what you need before you ask," Jesus says (Matt 6:8). The simplicity of the Lord's Prayer allows us to come before God in an authentic way, even when we have no other words. These are all the words we need.

Recite the Lord's Prayer. Go slowly and consider how your
understanding of the words has evolved.

THE FRIEND-
OF-A-FRIEND-OF-A-FRIEND

Lead me in your truth—teach it to me—because you are the God who saves me. I put my hope in you all day long.

—Psalm 25:5

Perhaps you've already encountered this situation—someone you know causally contacts you because he or she knows someone who knows someone with the same chronic illness as you and that someone has found a miracle cure. Have you tried it?

Unsolicited advice seems to come from everywhere once your diagnosis becomes public. While it's not always helpful, it is most often given with the best intentions in mind. And, I've found, it's most often given because those well-meaning folks don't know what else to do. Sometimes advice feels dismissive of what we're dealing with. The "all you have to do" kinds of advice remind me of Dorothy clicking her heels together to get home from Oz—rarely very helpful. It helps me to have a standard response, like "Thanks so much for thinking of me," or "I'll share that with my doctor," rather than discussing the pros and cons of (often uninformed) advice at length.

Anne Lamott writes, "Hope begins in the dark, the stubborn hope that if you just show up and try to do the right thing, the dawn will come. You wait and watch and work; you don't give up."[8] Our job is to wait and watch and work, not follow every piece of advice that is thrown at us. When we focus on our job, eventually, hope will come.

Lord, there is so much information to take in, so many decisions to be made. Sometimes I don't know which voices to listen to, which advice to take. Allow me, Lord, to hear the messages behind the advice—the offers hope, care, and love.

I WILL HOLD YOU IN MY HAND

Don't fear, because I am with you; don't be afraid, for I am your God.
I will strengthen you, I will surely help you; I will hold you with my
righteous strong hand.

—Isaiah 41:10

I am just a little tiny bit claustrophobic. I don't mind a sleeping bag or being packed in a car with my family, but there are some small places that are really scary for me. On the top of my list is an MRI machine. If you haven't had the opportunity to experience an MRI, let me tell you what you are missing: you lie on a narrow, cold bed in a cold room with your head wedged tight in a plastic cage and then are squeezed into a tiny hole surrounded by blinking lights and scary sounds...need I go on? It's difficult for me to stay calm during these tests. The last time I had one, tears of fear ran down my face as the technician was giving me the contrast dye. I was explaining that I knew my fear was irrational when he interrupted, asked if music would help, and showed me all the albums he had available. I picked out a soothing, familiar record and had the best MRI of my life.

That wasn't the first or last time that I felt fear and it wasn't the first or last time a stranger intervened to ease that fear. In Isaiah, the writer assures us that God is bigger than our fear. And God often sends those kind strangers to remind us that God "will surely help you." As you face fears on this journey, pray for the people you will encounter. Those prayers will strengthen you no matter how scary the sounds you are facing!

Take a few minutes for breath prayer. Breathe in "calm" and
breathe out "fear." Allow God to take that fear for you.

GRACE SUFFICIENT

Therefore, I'm all right with weaknesses, insults, disasters, harassments, and stressful situations for the sake of Christ, because when I'm weak, then I'm strong.

—2 Corinthians 12:10

One of the first songs that many of us remember learning is "Jesus Loves Me." What wonderful words to carry in our hearts! The lyrics "They are weak, but He is strong" are echoed in 2 Corinthians 12:9-10. Paul is sharing a vision he had with the new believers in Corinth and recalls the words that the Lord spoke to him "My grace is enough for you because power is made perfect in weakness" (v. 9). While we cannot all emulate Paul in taking pleasure in infirmities, we can take heart that our hardships can reveal the power of God.

During a children's sermon, my pastor was singing this song with the gathered children and leading the motions. I had to notice how much energy the kids put into the "strong" arm movement, flexing their little muscles with enthusiasm. Our society puts a lot more stock into strength than it does into weakness. Even children see that and know the importance of showing their own power. But as Christians, our real strength comes from allowing ourselves to be weak, knowing that true power and true wholeness comes only from God. When we find our bodies weakened with illness, we rest in the knowledge that God's grace and strength is sufficient for us.

Close your eyes as you sing aloud or in your mind the words to "Jesus Loves Me." Which of these lyrics do you need most right now? Remember that you belong to Jesus.

FOR WHEN YOU ARE WEARY

The Holy Spirit… will remind you of everything I told you.
Peace I leave with you. My peace I give you.
—John 14:26-27

struggle with fatigue and as I've learned to live with it, I can identify the many forms it takes. There is a deep, bone-level fatigue that keeps me from getting out of bed. There is a lesser fatigue that allows me to do "normal" things like grocery shopping, but I don't have the energy to run back to the dairy section if I've forgotten something. And there is the mental fatigue that comes from worry, stress, demanding schedules, and feeling burned out. Not to mention the emotional fatigue that comes with dealing with a chronic illness! When my body is wrung out, I can cope by resting, but when my soul feels hung out to dry, it takes God to knit me back together.

When fatigue overtakes me, and I feel weary down to my bones, I need the Holy Spirit. I think of songs like "Spirit of the Living God," where we ask the Holy Spirit to "fall afresh on me." Isn't that image wonderful? Maybe you think of it like a gentle rain falling upon and soothing your body. Perhaps it's more like the flames the disciples saw at Pentecost. The Holy Spirit is all about refreshing, renewing, and reigniting our fires. In your weariness, allow the Holy Spirit to enter your heart anew.

Use a breath prayer to speak the Holy Spirit into your soul. Choose two words that bring you peace and restoration. As you breathe in, pray one word. As you breathe out, pray the other. Take time to allow your breathing to become slow and relaxed. Give yourself time to listen to the Holy Spirit and just be.

CAST YOUR BREAD

I'm convinced that nothing can separate us from God's love in Christ Jesus our Lord: not death or life, not angels or rulers, not present things or future things, not powers or height or depth, or any other thing that is created.

—Romans 8:38-39

We once had a pastor who was able to see the positive and hold onto hope in amazing ways. When we were in a frustrating or stressful situation, my husband and I would play "What Would Pastor Mary Do?" imagining what her response might be. In a slow checkout line at the grocery? That cashier has been on her feet all day and was up with a sick baby all last night. Bless her heart, she's doing the best she can! Waiting on the results of an important medical test? No need to worry! God knows the answer before we do and has a plan all figured out! Her favorite saying for people in crisis was, "Cast your bread upon the water. God will butter and jam it and send it right back."

I readily admit that I don't have a "Pastor Mary attitude" all the time. It's easy to slip into a negativity, especially when you're not feeling well. I need these words from Romans to remind me that nothing, not even a bad attitude, can separate me from God. Even when it's difficult to see the silver lining or grasp for even a sliver of hope, God is with me. When I feel like a dark attitude is creeping in, I can cast my hope on the eternal love of God.

Nothing helps a bad attitude like music. What songs can pull you out of a funk? What is it about the lyrics, the music, the rhythm that cheer you up? Think about the music that lifts your spirit and restores hope, and listen to it, if possible!

THE POWER OF COMMUNITY

"Lord... when did we see you sick or in prison and visit you?"
Then the king will reply to them, "I assure you that when you have done it
for one of the least of these... you have done it for me.
—Matthew 25:39-40

We're all part of some kind of community, whether or not we are active members. Maybe you don't know your neighbors by name but you may have friends who gather at the local coffee shop. You may not be on all the committees at church, but you probably know who in the congregation will be there for you when you need them. As we go through life, our needs for community changes. With a difficult diagnosis this is even truer—you need your people! Community offers moral support, laughter, care, and sometimes even casseroles . . . things we all need from time to time.

Needing help is not unique to those of us living with chronic illness. Still, even though it's universal, asking for help is hard. When we ask for help, we are admitting that we cannot meet a need by ourselves. We may feel embarrassed or even ashamed. Think of a time that someone needed you. Perhaps you took a meal to a family with a new child or gave someone a ride to an appointment. Didn't it feel good to know that you could help even in a small way? Asking for help and allowing others to help is part of being in the beloved community of Christ.

Lord, help me overcome the barriers that keep me from engaging
more fully in my community. Give me your grace in my
vulnerability. Thank you for giving us the gift of community. Amen.

ARE YOU BETTER TODAY?

We put our hope in the LORD. He is our help and shield.
—Psalm 33:20

When someone is sick with a cold or virus, he or she generally starts feeling better after taking medication or taking time to rest. Chronic illnesses are different; that's why they are "chronic." It can get annoying to have people check in daily to see if you're "better yet"! It can be difficult to hold onto hope, when you are reminding folks that, no, you aren't better. Thich Nhat Hanh writes, "Hope is important because it can make the present moment less difficult to bear. If we believe that tomorrow will be better, we can bear a hardship today."[9]

Years ago, my mother suggested to the kids some ways they could help when I was feeling badly, like getting me a drink of water. One day my preschool-aged son found me on the couch with multiple heating pads and ran to "help." He brought me the only glass he could reach—the one he used after brushing his teeth—filled to the brim with tepid bathroom water. He held onto the grimy, toothpaste-smeared cup and balanced it carefully across the living room, so proud of himself. As I drank the precious gift he'd brought me, he expectantly raised his eyebrows and asked, "Better?" He definitely made that present moment less difficult to bear and made me feel loved and cared for. Even if my body wasn't "better," my spirit was.

Lord, open my heart to the small gifts of comfort that surround me.
Help me see your hope in them. Amen.

REMEMBER TO PLAY

Your eyes saw my embryo, and on your scroll every day was written that was being formed for me, before any one of them had yet happened. God, your plans are incomprehensible to me! Their total number is countless!
—Psalm 139:16-17

As a kid, I loved playgrounds. When I think back to the joy and excitement that filled my heart upon seeing a new place to play, I can barely recall what was behind my eager anticipation. There wasn't just one part of a playground that I liked; it was all good: swings, slides, monkey bars, climbing, exploring. So much of that type of play is about learning new physical skills and testing one's courage. Now, as I often have to learn new physical skills due to a chronic illness it's difficult to find the joy I once had for these feats. I'm no longer eager to move my body and try new things. I'm more interested in conserving my movements to avoid injury!

In Psalm 139, David prays for deliverance from his enemies and begins by recounting his own creation. Like David, God saw us as embryos and has ordered our days. We were marvelously and fearfully created by a loving God who has planned for us for eternity. Even though we may feel disconnected from our bodies as we struggle with chronic illness, our physical bodies are still good and whole in God's eyes. Think about some physical activity that brought you joy as a child. You may not be capable of that activity, but you are able recall the joy that our bodies have brought us. Thanks be to God.

Close your eyes and think about your favorite childhood activity. Think about the sounds and smells that you associate with those memories. As you are able, stretch your limbs and imagine the new ways your body can honor God with joy.

SIMPLE GIFTS

Every good gift, every perfect gift, comes from above. These gifts come down from the Father, the creator of the heavenly lights, in whose character there is no change at all.

—James 1:17

A few years ago, a close friend of mine contracted a flesh-eating bacteria. She underwent multiple surgeries to rid her of the infected tissue and endured weeks of wound care that left her weak and in a lot of pain. During this time, her family rallied around her in many amazing ways, but I'll never forget the day I went to visit and found her husband in the kitchen. He was busily arranging some melon slices around a little mound of cottage cheese. His wife was having a hard time eating; her appetite was bad and nothing appealed to her. So, he was trying to make every meal beautiful, carefully carving the melon slices to resemble petals of a flower around their cottage cheese center. It was an act of tenderness and love, of care and hope.

We may not all have partners who make us melon flowers, but our loved ones let us know they care in many ways. As we experience chronic illness, those around us experience it, too. From their perspective, it might be frightening or confusing. It may cause some to step back, not knowing what to do. Others may jump at every chance to help and become overwhelming. But watch for the simple gifts, the little times our people extend their love in their own way. We can easily overlook these acts, forgetting that these gestures of tenderness, love, care, and hope are offerings of God's love.

Take time to thank God for those who extend simple gifts of love and help to you.

FILLING UP YOUR RESERVES

Those who stand firm during testing are blessed. They are tried and true.
They will receive the life God has promised
to those who love him as their reward.

—*James 1:12*

Traditionally, scholars have believed that the book of James was written by Jesus's brother, James. He's writing to small and scattered communities of believers, offering moral direction and encouragement. How difficult it would have been to keep your faith going in such a time and place! Throughout the book, he acknowledges the trials that these early followers of Christ were experiencing.

How can we apply these words from James to our journey with chronic illness? It's not always as easy as turning a frown upside-down. We need to create and sustain reserves of faith for this journey. We need to cultivate places where we tuck away the promises God has made, so we can pull them out when we need them most. We listen and learn our heart's song so that on those days when there is no song in our heart, we can sing it anyway. Like a pilot filling up the extra fuel tanks for a long flight, we fill up our faith tanks for all we will encounter. On days that are good, we soak in the joy, we make memories, we offer thanks. On days that are bad, we can rejoice in those memories and remember the feelings of joy and gratitude. We can find a song to sing and stand firm.

〰〰〰〰〰〰〰〰〰〰〰〰〰〰〰〰〰〰〰〰〰〰〰〰〰

How can we cultivate a song in our hearts when we can't find one
there? If today is a good day, work on it now: think of a song that
has significant meaning to you. What is it about that piece that
moves you? Does it bring with it special memories or relationships?
Offer God thanks.

〰〰〰〰〰〰〰〰〰〰〰〰〰〰〰〰〰〰〰〰〰〰〰〰〰

POSSIBILITIES

> *It's easier for a camel to squeeze through the eye of a needle
> than for a rich person to enter God's kingdom.*
>
> —Matthew 19:24

Since my diagnosis, I've made decisions that I now regret. Most of these decisions were things I didn't do because I just didn't think they were possible. Travel to a place that requires lots of walking? Surely I can't do that. Take on a new job that requires lots of stamina? I don't know that I have it in me! Feeling that so many things were outside the realm of possibility for me left me feeling fragile, disconnected, and fearful. I'd always seen myself as brave and courageous, and my sense of self was at an all-time low. Many things felt outside of my control and as impossible as fitting a camel through the eye of a needle.

In Matthew 19, the disciples are asking Jesus about who will be able to enter the kingdom of heaven. It's in verse 28 that we hear the familiar words, "It is impossible for human beings. But all things are possible with God." Just what I needed to remember when I was giving up! I had been so focused on *me* and what *I* could and couldn't do I had not allowed God into the equation. I had lost my trust in the Lord. Once I put God's presence and power back into the equation, I found myself doing things that felt impossible—but weren't. By reclaiming my place as a child of God, I was able to dwell once again in possibility.

Loving God, I know I can do far more through you than I can on my own. My limits are not your limits. Take me by the hand and lead me on, regardless of my fears or assumptions. Amen.

YOUR NEW NORMAL

You are the one who lights my lamp.
The LORD my God illuminates my darkness.

—Psalm 18:28

Our world really loves the word *normal*. It encompasses all that is expected and all that is acceptable. When I ask them how their school day was, my kids usually say, "Like normal." But I haven't been with them at school. I don't know what their idea of "normal" looks like! Are they struggling through their lessons and eating lunch alone? Their idea of normal may not be the same as mine.

The same is true with the "normal" we are living in with chronic disease. Your normal may have more prescriptions and appointments than it once did. It may include new habits and more accommodations than it once did. It probably looks very different from the world's idea of what is expected and acceptable.

Tortured artist Vincent van Gogh, who likely suffered from some form of chronic mental illness, is credited for saying, "Normality is a paved road. It's comfortable to walk, but no flowers grow on it." As difficult as the journey of chronic illness is, you will find the flowers that grow only here. There will be new friendships, new experiences, and new understandings of self. It won't always or even often be a comfortable walk, but you will find unexpected joy. You may be off of the paved road but you aren't travelling alone. You take with you your hope, your community, and your God. Allow yourself the grace to travel this road with hope knowing that God illuminates your path.

Ever-present God, the road before me is not the one I expected to take. Guide me as I process the grief of what might have been and embrace the extraordinary, unusual beauty of what is. I trust that you will bring me through even my darkest days. Amen.

NOTES

1. WHAT IS CHRONIC ILLNESS?

1. Stephanie Bernell and Stephen W. Howard, "Use Your Words Carefully: What Is Chronic Disease?" Frontiers in Public Health, August 2, 2016, www.ncbi.nlm.nih.gov/pmc/articles/PMC4969287/.

2. "About Chronic Diseases," National Health Council fact sheet, 2014, www.nationalhealthcouncil.org/sites/default/files/NHC_Files/Pdf_Files/About ChronicDisease.pdf.

4. LIVING YOUR BEST LIFE

1. Elaine Smookler, "Beginner's Body Scan Meditation," Mindful, March 10, 2016, www.mindful.org/beginners-body-scan-meditation/.

2. Ann Voskamp, "What the Church and Christians Need to Know about Suicide and Mental Health," Huffington Post, October 14, 2014, www.huffingtonpost.com/ann-voskamp/what-the-church-and-chris_b_5676318.html.

DEVOTIONS

1. Rachel Held Evans, *A Year of Biblical Womanhood* (Nashville: Thomas Nelson, 2012), 188.

2. "The Most Optimistic Guy in Hollywood," Beliefnet, 2009, www.beliefnet.com/entertainment/celebrities/2009/05/michael-j-fox-interview.aspx.

3. Alice Walker, *The Color Purple* (New York: Houghton Mifflin Harcourt, 1992), 196.

4. Mary Oliver, *Swan: Poems and Prose Poems* (Boston: Beacon Press, 2012), 42.

5. John Lennon, lyrics for The Beatles, "I Get By with a Little Help from My Friends," *Sgt. Pepper's Lonely Hearts Club Band* (Hollywood: Capitol Records, 1967).

6. Henri Nouwen, "Introduction to the 1980 Edition" of Parker Palmer's The

Promise of Paradox: A Celebration of Contradictions in the Christian Life (San Francisco: Jossey-Bass, 1980), ix.

7. C. S. Lewis, *Mere Christianity* (New York: HarperCollins, 1980), 125.

8. Anne Lamott, *Bird by Bird: Some Instructions on Writing and Life* (New York: Anchor Books, 1995), xxiii.

9. Thich Nhat Hanh, *Peace Is Every Step: The Path of Mindfulness in Everyday Life* (New York: Bantam, 1992), 41.